Adopted and Wondering

Drawing Out Feelings

Written by Marge Eaton Heegaard

To be illustrated by children
to help families communicate and learn together

Fairview Press
Minneapolis

Published by Fairview Press, 2450 Riverside Avenue, Minneapolis, Minnesota 55454.
Fairview Press is a division of Fairview Health Services, a community-focused health system affiliated
with the University of Minnesota and providing a complete range of services, from the prevention of
illness and injury to care for the most complex medical conditions. For a free current catalog of Fairview
Press titles, please call toll-free 1-800-544-8207. Or visit our Web site at http://www.fairviewpress.org.

ISBN: 978-1-57749-166-8

First Printing: February 2007
Printed in the United States

Cover design by Laurie Ingram
Interior by Dorie McClelland, Spring Book Design

For their expertise and input, we gratefully acknowledge the following professionals: Louise A.
Fleischman, LCSW-C, Center for Adoptive Families; Christopher J. Alexander, Ph.D.; Lauren Zeek,
M.Ed. LPC, CT; Jennifer Wilson and the staff of the Children's Home Society and Family Services; Debby
Riley, Executive Director, Center for Adoption Support and Education. We also acknowledge the
contributions of those who have personally experienced adoption as a child, parent, or grandparent: Mary
Berdan; Joe Carrol; Joe Callihan; Bev Maxwell; Bob Pool; Ann Butts; Barbara Eckholdt; Lucina Slaten.

About this book.

This book is designed for children ages 6-12 who were adopted. Ideally, it should be used with a parent or an adult trained to work with children. Before giving the book to a child, the adult needs to read the book to be familiar with its content.

Most children like to do about 5 pages at a time, once or twice a week. Allow children to illustrate their book with pictures they choose to draw as they read the words on each page. Children are often better able to share difficult experiences and concerns with pictures than words.

While children may need help in understanding some of the words and concepts in this book, adults can encourage them to make their own decisions about what to draw or write. This provides a sense of empowerment.

Some children may prefer to use markers, but crayons can be more expressive. Older children may use colored pencils and add more words. Help children focus on expressing thoughts and feelings rather than on drawing ability.

The art process allows children to express personal feelings symbolically. They may choose to skip a page that is still too painful to deal with. An adult should be available to invite children to share more about their pictures and to listen carefully to understand what they are experiencing.

As children learn to understand adoption and to communicate their concerns, they will heal early misconceptions and develop important life lessons for coping with loss and change.

Parents and other adults can make a difference.

Parents need to talk to their adopted children early on but especially before the teen years when children begin to ask the question, "Who am I?" This is when the emotional impact of wondering may come to adopted children. To prevent later difficulties, ages 6–12 may be the best years to talk about and work with children about any adoption concerns they may have.

Adoption is different for every child, depending on age at time of placement, experiences prior to adoption, and other issues. Young children often see themselves as a mirror of a parent. It helps them if they can think of their birth parents as people who may have loved them but were unable to give them a home. Allow children to have respect for the woman who gave them life. Questions about birth mothers usually come before questions about birth fathers, but both are important in building a child's sense of identity.

Children need to know it is OK to think and talk about their adoption. And adults need to let children know they are interested as well. Just because children are not asking questions does not mean that they are not wondering about their adoption. When children do ask questions, they need answers that are meaningful and age-appropriate.

Adoption can be difficult for children to understand. They may wonder why they couldn't stay with their birth family. Was something wrong with them? Did they do something wrong? They may wonder if their birth parent will try to reclaim them. They may wonder if their adoptive parents will always want to keep them. They may develop fantasies about things that never happened. They may believe they came from bad people and, therefore, are bad themselves. They may act out in unhealthy ways.

Adoption is a life-altering event—a change that can create loss and grief as well as joy. If these feelings are not addressed, children can develop problems with identity, trust, control, self-esteem, and intimacy.

Children may grieve in silence. They may not talk about any grief, but their drawings and their actions may. Regression, hyperactivity, physical complaints, and angry outbreaks may be signs of grieving, not misbehaving.

Not every child will experience loss the same way. Some are OK with the adoption and feel no need to know more—at least, for the time being. Some children may deny the reality of their loss and cover grief by being "perfect" or angry and controlling. They may distance themselves emotionally or physically from others to avoid rejection and further loss.

As excited and happy as adoptive parents may be, children may have very different feelings. In international adoptions, even very young children may react to the strange new smells, foods, and voices with feelings of anxiety. Children may feel confused, angry, or sad, and they may act out difficult feelings they do not know how to express.

Feelings of loss and abandonment affect not only a child's behavior but also their emotional growth and development. Adopted children need to understand their feelings before they can be fully comforted.

Children who express negative feelings about being adopted when they are grieving may later come to appreciate the parents who raised them. Adults can help children understand and accept their losses. They cannot make their losses smaller, but they can make their lives greater. The most important life-long task for adoptive parents may be to integrate their children's separate biographies—their "forever" families, their foster families, and their adoptive families.

This book uses the art process to help children learn to:

To children

This is your book. You will make it different from all other books by drawing your own thoughts and feelings. You do not need any special skills to do this. Just draw the pictures that come into your head as you read the words on each page.

Begin with the first page and do the pages in order. Ask an adult for help with words or pages you do not understand. When you have done a few pages, stop and share your work with an adult who cares about you.

Drawing pictures can make it easier to talk about things you may have been wondering about in silence. Sharing concerns with others can help you feel better about yourself and others.

I hope you will enjoy this book as you learn to understand and express your feelings. My grandmother was adopted as a small child, and I wrote this book for you in honor of her.

To "adopt" means to choose as one's own. More than 100,000 children are adopted in the U.S. each year.

(Draw a picture that you could call "Adoption," and list the names of people you know who were adopted.)

Adoption is an important relationship. Children need a family, and families need children to love and care for.

It is not easy for a birth mother to place her child for adoption. She may feel sad that she cannot watch her child grow up. She may feel angry that she cannot keep her child. She may feel guilty that she is unable to care for her child.

(Draw a picture of how you think your birth mother felt.)

There are many reasons why birth parents cannot take care of a child. They may be not be old enough, have enough money, or be physically or mentally capable. Often, they want their child to have a better life than they feel they could give.

Before a child is adopted, a placement agency works hard to find a home where the child will be loved and given the best care. Parents may have to wait a long time for a child.

(Draw a picture of how your parents felt while they waited to adopt you.)

Many people want to adopt a child.

When adults are told there is a child who needs a family, they feel happy and excited.

(Draw a picture of how your parents felt when they learned they could adopt you.)

Adoption is an agreement in which the birth parents pass their parental rights and responsibilities to the adoptive parents.

Children of all ages may have lived in different places before being adopted.

____ in the hospital they were born in
____ in the birth parents' home
____ in a foster home
____ in an orphanage
____ in a different country far away
____ other _____

(Check ✓ where you think you've been and draw or write about it.)

You are an important part of your family, and the story of how you joined your family is important, too.

When a home is not a safe place or parents are unable to care for a child, the child may live in a foster family or orphanage until a permanent home can be found. Some children live in more than one foster home before they are adopted.

(Draw a picture of an orphanage or your foster family, if you had one. Or draw a picture of a child waiting to be adopted.)

Foster parents may have many foster children they love, but are unable to adopt them for many different reasons.

Many children are adopted from a different state or country far away.

(Write or draw what you know about the place you came from.)

The United States is called the "melting pot" because so many different people have come here from so many different countries.

I was _____ years old when my family adopted me. Sometimes children must be placed by birth mothers in a safe place where they can be taken care of until they are adopted.

(Draw yourself and a place you may have been placed.)

You would have felt very frightened and helpless if this happened to you. You may still feel this way sometimes.

Young children cannot take care of themselves. They have different ways of getting what they want.

(Draw a picture of what you did as a young child to get what you wanted.)

Young children often cry, yell, or hit. A little child is still inside you. But crying, yelling, or hitting won't work as you get older. Words become more effective.

I wonder what my life would have been like if I had not been adopted.

(Draw a picture of what you think might have happened.)

Adoption is confusing. Some children may wish they had just one mom or dad. It helps to draw and talk about the things you wonder about.

I have been told I was adopted because _____

_____

_____

_____

_____

But sometimes I think I may have been adopted
because I _____

_____

_____

_____

Adoption is an adult thing. It is not because of
something children do or do not do.

I do not want to hurt my parents' feelings, but I would like to talk about some of the things I wonder and worry about.

(Write about or draw your worries.)

Your parents are always concerned about anything that worries you. They can support you and find any help you need.

Many children wonder if their birth parents are still alive and if their birth parents still think about them. I sometimes wonder . . .

(Finish this sentence with words or pictures.)

It is OK to be interested in your birth parents and to ask questions.

Some children seem to have no interest in their lives before adoption. I am / am not interested because . . .

_____

_____

_____

_____

You may begin to wonder and have more questions about your adoption as you get older. It is OK to wonder.

Change is part of living. Adoption brings change. It is often a good change, but with change there is also loss, and loss can bring feelings called GRIEF.

Feelings of grief may come and go like ocean wave before healing comes. It may be hard to feel anything at first. This is called DENIAL. Nothing feels real. When feelings do come, they can be difficult and confusing. Drawing pictures may help you express your feelings more easily.

Times of loss and change can lead to growth and strength. Recognizing, understanding, and sharing feelings strengthens present relationships.

Feelings are called feelings because you feel them someplace in your body.

(Think of a time when you had a strong feeling. Choose a color and show where you felt that feeling. Scribble that color next to the word it goes with.)

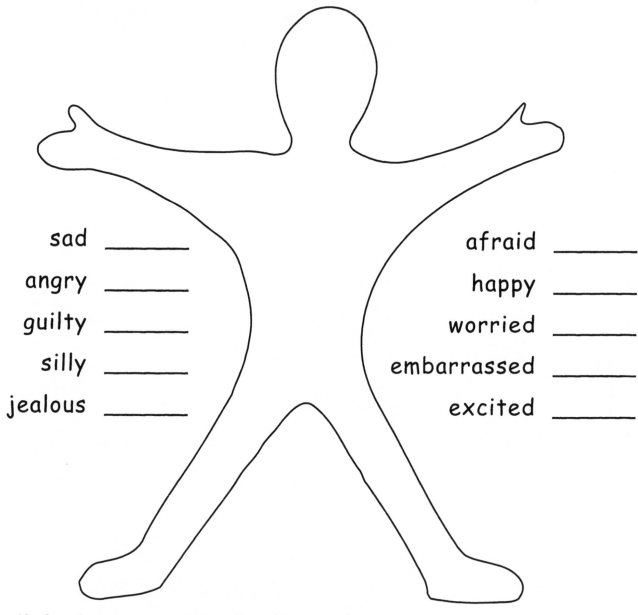

sad _____

angry _____

guilty _____

silly _____

jealous _____

afraid _____

happy _____

worried _____

embarrassed _____

excited _____

All feelings are OK. Feelings change.

There are many good ways to let feelings out.

(Check ✓ what you do.)

___ Paint with watercolors.
___ Write in a journal or diary.
___ Draw pictures.
___ Exercise or play sports.
___ Walk or run.
___ Shout into a pillow.
___ Play a musical instrument or sing.
___ Clean my room.
___ Say "I am feeling . . . "
___ Play with my toys or games.
___ Tear up old newspapers.
___ Do something nice for someone.
___ Other ways you let out feelings:

Feelings just happen. But you can choose how you behave.

When I get angry, I . . .

(Draw a picture of what you do when you feel angry.)

It's OK to feel angry, but it is not OK to hurt people or things.

I feel sad when . . .

(Finish the sentence with words or a picture.)

Your parents would like to comfort you when you feel sad, but sometimes your inside feelings don't show on the outside.

Anxiety is the fear of not being able to cope with something you think might happen.

(Draw a picture you would call "Anxiety.")

I have anxiety when _____

_____

Many children feel anxious in times of separation and loss. It helps to talk to someone about this.

When I feel lonely, I . . .

(Draw a picture of what you do when you feel lonely.)

Some children avoid feeling close to others because they are afraid of being rejected. But it is important to have family, friends, and people you can trust to be there for you. Learning more about your life before adoption can help you recognize and understand any feelings you may have.

Another woman besides my adopted mother gave birth to me. She is my birth, or first, mother.

(Draw a picture of how your birth mother may have looked.)

Your adoptive parents are glad that your first mother loved you enough to give you life. They will now help you learn how to live your life.

A different man than my adopted father helped to create me. He is called my birth, or first, father.

(Draw a picture of how you think your birth father may have looked.)

Some birth fathers never know that they have helped to create a child. Or they may feel sad and guilty that they were unable to give their child a good life.

Some people call birth parents their "real" parents, but your adoptive parents have the legal right and responsibility to take care of you. Both birth parents and adoptive parents are real parents.

(Draw a picture of your adoptive family.)

Blood lines and love lines are both important, but love is more important for helping children grow up to be good and happy adults.

Sometimes I feel different from others in my family because . . .

(Write or draw about the ways you may feel different.)

Differences are interesting. They are often good and need to be respected.

Children inherit some physical characteristics and natural talents from their birth parents.

(List or draw some things about yourself that may have come from your birth parents.)

You can be proud of these things. You may pass them on to your children some day.

Character traits, such as being kind, respectful, honest, fair, grateful, and responsible, are taught to children by the parents they live with.

(Write down some of the good things your parents are teaching you.)

You could grow up to be a parent yourself some day.

My life is not always easy, but I am glad that I am alive, and I want to thank my first parents for giving me life.

(Write a thank-you note to your birth parents.)

Your first parents would be proud of the child you have grown up to be. They would be happy that your adopted parents have been able to do more for you than they were able to do.

I may want to hear more of the story of my birth and early life as I grow older. I may want to learn about . . .

(Finish this sentence with words or a picture.)

Questions can be asked and answered at different stages of life. Besides the support of family and friends, you may find books, support groups, or counseling helpful.

I have my own talents and abilities, and I have ideas of what I want to do in the future.

(Draw yourself as an adult doing something important.)

Many people care about and love you. You can help make the world a better place.

Change brings good as well as loss. I want to celebrate my adoption and my family.

(Draw or write something about how you would celebrate your adoption.)

Being in a family means being loved and cared for by parents. It also means giving love and care to others.

Made in the USA
Middletown, DE
26 March 2017